MW01703640

Minute Meditations

Minute Meditations

CARL F. PELTZ

Pauline
BOOKS & MEDIA
BOSTON

ISBN 0-8198-4779-8

Cover design by Helen Rita Lane, FSP

Printed in Korea

Published by Pauline Books & Media, 50 St. Paul's Avenue, Boston, MA 02130.

Pauline Books & Media is the publishing house of the Daughters of St. Paul, an international congregation of women religious serving the Church with the communications media.

1 2 3 4 99 98 97 96

Introduction

As a busy person, you have no time to waste. Countless tasks crowd your calendar. You may even think that it's a bother to read this introduction.

This booklet is not intended to condemn you for being busy. There are probably some good and even noble reasons why you have so little time for yourself. Rather, this booklet can help you find time for God in the midst of a busy life.

The Gospels portray Jesus Christ as giving many calls to his first disciples. They were called to baptize, to celebrate the Eucharist, to forgive, to love one another, to proclaim the Good News, to reconcile and to serve. However, Jesus Christ initially called the disciples to spend time with him before he called them to do anything else. Responding to this call was fundamental to being a genuine disciple of Jesus Christ.

Jesus Christ is calling you to be a disciple. Like the first disciples, you are primarily called to find ways by which you can be in the Lord' presence. Responding to this call involves energy and time. Hopefully, you have the energy. However, you simply may not have much free time to yourself. Yet, in the busyness of your life, our Lord still calls out to you, "Come, spend some time with me!"

This booklet was written to help you spend some quality time being with Jesus Christ in a direct and uncomplicated manner. It contains a total of sixty meditations. Each meditation will take about one minute to complete and is intended to be used on a different day.

The meditations focus on specific topics and each one contains a short reflection, followed by a question for the day. As you move through the reflections you will discover that they contain some simple yet real pathways to the Lord Jesus. You will also find the reflections short and to the point. They will provide you with a single thought for each day. The questions are directed toward your own experiences and they will help you profit from the reflections.

A minute a day is a small amount of time to give to such an important endeavor as our response to discipleship. However, your task in using this booklet is not quantity. It is quality! Besides, when you have finished this booklet, you will have spent at least one hour trying to be with Jesus Christ. The Gospels portray the Master as being able to do some wonderful things with his first disciples in that amount of time.

The topics for the meditations have been drawn from certain Gospel passages. The particular passage for each meditation is presented before the reflection. You may consider reading the passage if you find yourself being able to give more than one minute of private time to the Lord Jesus.

Reformation

After John was arrested, Jesus came into Galilee proclaiming the good news of God and saying, "The appointed time has been fulfilled and the Kingdom of God is at hand; repent and believe in the good news!" As he was walking along the Sea of Galilee he saw Simon and Simon's brother Andrew casting throw nets into the sea—they were fishermen. Jesus said to them, "Follow me, and I'll make you fishers of men!" And they left their nets at once and followed him. He continued on a little way and saw James son of Zebedee and his brother, John—they were in the boat mending the nets. He called them at once, and they left their father Zebedee in the boat with the hired men and followed him (Mk 1:14-20).

We need to stop playing God, if we are to find God.

As disciples, we need to examine our lives in order to identify the different ways we try to play God. We have not been called to be all-knowing, all-powerful or perfect in any way. Rather, we have been called to grow in our faith. We need to focus on those activities and practices that will help us believe that Jesus Christ is truly with us. Then our faith can empower us to deal with life as we go about the business of the day.

Today's Question

What is one way that I am trying to play God in my life?

Little Things

After this Jesus went off to the other side of the Sea of Galilee of Tiberias. A large crowd was following him because they saw the signs he was performing on the sick. So Jesus went up the mountain and sat down there with his disciples. Now the Passover, the festival of the Jews, was near. When Jesus raised his eyes and saw that a large crowd was coming toward him he said to Philip, "Where can we buy loaves for them to eat?" He said this to test him—he knew what he was going to do. Philip answered him, "Two hundred denarii worth of bread wouldn't be enough to allow each of them to have a little!" One of his disciples, Andrew, Simon Peter's brother, said to him, "There's a boy here who has five barley loaves and two fish, but what are they for so many?" Jesus said, "Have the people sit down"—now there was a lot of grass at that spot. So the men, numbering about five thousand, sat down. Jesus took the loaves and after blessing them he distributed them to those who were reclining, and likewise with the fish, as much as they wanted. When they were full he said to his disciples,

"Gather the left-over fragments so nothing will be lost." So they gathered them and filled twelve baskets with fragments of the five barley loaves which were left by those who had eaten. When the people saw the sign he'd done they said, "Truly this is the prophet who is to come into the world!" But when Jesus realized that they intended to come and take him by force to make him king he withdrew alone to the mountain again (Jn 6:1-15).

Jesus Christ is able to accomplish great things through the little things we give him.

We can't always give to prayer as much time as we would like. We can't always approach Jesus Christ with a clear mind and a focused heart. Sometimes, all we can do is believe that Jesus Christ can reveal his abiding presence through the little pieces of self which we give him. So, let's lighten up on ourselves and work at putting more trust in the one we call "Lord."

Today's Question

What is one little piece of self that I can realistically give to my Lord?

Plans

After leaving the synagogue he went to Simon and Andrew's house with James and John. Peter's mother-in-law was burning with fever, and at once they told Jesus about her. He went over to her, grasped her hand and raised her up, and the fever left her and she began to serve them. When it was evening, when the sun had set, they brought him all the people who were sick and were demon-possessed, and the whole city was gathered at the door. He cured many who were sick with all kinds of diseases and drove out many demons, and he didn't allow the demons to speak, because they knew him. Early in the morning, long before daylight, he got up, went out, and went off to a desert place, and there he prayed. Simon and those with him tracked him down and when they found him they said to him, "Everyone's looking for you!" He said to them, "Let's go elsewhere, to the neighboring country towns, so I can preach there as well—this is what I came for!" And he went through all Galilee, preaching in their synagogues and driving out demons (Mk 1:29-39).

The most obvious course of action is not always the best course of action. Rather, the best course of action is the one that enables us to complete whatever needs to be done in a given day.

We begin to walk the same path as Jesus Christ whenever we set out to do whatever really needs to be done during the course of a given day. When we are willing to take the path Jesus Christ is walking, we may even be surprised to discover how he connects himself to us through the work that fills our day.

Today's Question

What is one thing that I need to do today?

Refrainment

A leper came up to him, begging him and kneeling down and saying to him, "If you wish to, you can make me clean!" Greatly moved, Jesus reached out his hand, touched him, and said to him, "I *do* wish it; be made clean!" and at once the leprosy left him and he was made clean. After admonishing him Jesus at once sent him away, saying to him, "See that you tell no one, but go show yourself to the priest and offer for your cleansing what Moses commanded, as a witness to them." But the man went out and began to spread the word and proclaim it so energetically that Jesus wasn't even able to enter a city openly; instead, he stayed out in desert places, and people would come to him from all directions (Mk 1:40-45).

At times, the important thing is not what we do or say. Rather, what matters is what we refrain from doing or saying.

As disciples, we need to remember how refrainment, in some circumstances, can be an action that allows the Lord to reveal something of his abiding presence.

Today's Question

What is one thing that I want to do or say which might be better off left undone or unsaid?

Experience

He came into Capharnaum again a few days later, and it became known that he was at home. So many people gathered around that there was no longer room even in front of the door, and he spoke the word to them. Then some people came to him carrying a paralytic, borne by four men. And since they couldn't bring him through to Jesus because of the crowd, they removed the roof where Jesus was, and after opening it up they lowered the cot on which the paralytic was laid. When Jesus saw their faith he said to the paralytic, "Child, your sins are forgiven!" Some of the scribes were seated there and they questioned in their hearts, "How can the fellow talk like that? He's blaspheming! Who but God alone is able to forgive sins?" Jesus realized at once in his spirit that they were questioning within themselves in this way, and so he said to them, "Why are you questioning these things in your hearts? What's easier, to say to the paralytic, 'Your sins are forgiven,' or to say, 'Get up, pick up your cot, and walk?' But so you'll know that the Son of Man has authority to forgive sins on earth"—he said to the paralytic, "I say to you, get up, pick up your cot, and go to your house!" And he got up, picked up his cot at once and went out in full sight of everyone, causing everyone to be amazed and to glorify God, saying, "We've never seen anything like this!" (Mk 2:1-12)

As disciples, listening to the Gospel of Jesus Christ takes a priority in our lives. To listen to the words contained in the Gospels nourishes our faith. However, at times words are simply not enough. Sometimes we need to experience the difference that the Gospel can bring about in people's lives. These experiences empower us to believe.

Today's Question

What is one thing that I can do or one place that I can go so as to experience the difference the Gospel can make?

Demons of Self

They entered Capharnaum, and he went into the synagogue and taught on the Sabbath. The people were amazed at the way he taught, for he was teaching them on his own authority, unlike the scribes. And there was a man with an unclean spirit in the synagogue who cried out, "What do you want with us, Jesus of Nazareth? Have you come to destroy us? I know who you are—the Holy One of God!" Jesus rebuked him and said, "Be silenced and come out of him!" And after throwing him into convulsions and crying out with a loud voice, the unclean spirit came out of him. Those gathered there were so astounded that they began to argue with one another and say, "What's going on? A new teaching given on his authority; he even gives orders to the unclean spirits, and they obey him!" And word of him went out everywhere in the whole district of Galilee (Mk 1:21-28).

Sometimes, the attitudes and behaviors that flow from a desire for self-actualization, self-fulfillment or self-realization are nothing less than demons of self which raise their ugly heads. Atti-

tudes and behaviors become demons when they spring from pride. Such attitudes and behaviors keep us so centered on ourselves that we cannot connect with the events of life taking place outside us. They keep us so focused on what we believe we can do for ourselves that they prevent us from recognizing our need for Jesus Christ in this life.

The Gospel of Jesus Christ can speak to the demons of self with a power that can cast them from us. However, we need to bring our demons out of their dark and hidden places. We need to bring them forth into the light by facing them and taking ownership of them. In doing so, we give the Gospel the opportunity to speak to our demons and break their power over us.

Today's Question

What is one demon that I need to face so that the Gospel can speak to it?

Openness

Once again he went into the synagogue. Now a man was there who had a withered hand and they were watching closely to see whether Jesus would heal him on the Sabbath, so they could make an accusation against him. So he said to the man with the withered hand, "Stand out in the middle." Then he said to them, "Which is lawful on the Sabbath, to do good or to do evil, to save a life or to kill?" But they remained silent. And after looking around at them in anger, deeply grieved at the hardness of their hearts, he said to the man, "Hold out your hand." The man held his hand out and it was restored. Then the Pharisees went out with the Herodians and began to plot to do away with Jesus (Mk 3:1-6).

We have not been called to know everything. Life is not a problem we try to solve. Rather, we have been called to accept life as a mystery in which Jesus Christ is now present.

As disciples, we need to guard ourselves against becoming closed to the different or the new in life. Openness can help us find some-

thing of the Christ who walks with us in the mystery of life.

Today's Question

What is one thing that I can do that will help me maintain an openness to life?

Withdrawing

Jesus departed with his disciples for the sea. A large crowd from Galilee followed and, having heard all he was doing, a large crowd as well from Judea and from Jerusalem and from Idumea and beyond the Jordan and around Tyre and Sidon came to him. He told his disciples to ready a small boat for him because of the crowd, so they wouldn't crush him— he was curing so many that those who had diseases pressed close upon him so they could touch him. As soon as the unclean spirits saw him they'd fall down before him and cry out, "You're the Son of God!" And he'd sternly command them not to make him known (Mk 3:7-12).

We have been called to become part of other people's lives. However, times will arise when we will also be called to withdraw from individuals or groups.

We need to be ready to remove ourselves from other people, if only for a short time, when they attempt to press themselves or their unsolicited agendas on us. Such distancing can even provide

Jesus Christ with the space he needs to make his presence more pronounced in our lives.

Today's Question

Is there someone or some group that I need to withdraw from, so that I can experience the Christ who dwells in me?

Fasting

John's disciples and the Pharisees were fasting, and people came and said to Jesus, "Why are John's disciples and the disciples of the Pharisees fasting, but your disciples aren't fasting?" Jesus said to them, "Can the groomsmen fast while the bridegroom is with them? As long as the bridegroom is with them they cannot fast, but the days will come when the bridegroom will be taken from them, and then, on that day, they'll fast. No one sews a patch of unshrunken cloth onto an old cloak, otherwise, the patch tears away from it, the new from the old, and the tear becomes worse. And no one puts new wine into old skins, otherwise, the wine will burst the skins, and both wine and skins are ruined; on the contrary, 'new wine in new skins'" (Mk 2:18-22).

Fasting does not celebrate the presence of Jesus Christ in our lives. Rather, it provides a way for us to express how we feel when we experience his absence.

The Kingdom of God is not yet complete. We do not always experience the felt presence of Jesus

Christ in our lives. Instead, we bump into our own limitations and the imperfections in our world. As hard as we try to find Jesus Christ in our lives, at times we experience his absence. This is the reality of the here and now.

Fasting enables us to express our experiences of the absent Christ. It enables us to connect with an important aspect of our reality.

Today's Question

When was the last time that I felt Jesus Christ was nowhere to be found?

Risks

It happened that as he was going through the grain fields on the Sabbath his disciples began plucking the heads of the grain as they made their way through. And the Pharisees said to him, "Look! Why are they doing what's unlawful on the Sabbath?" He said to them, "Haven't you ever read what David did when *he* was in need and was hungry, as well as those with him? How he went into the house of God when Abiathar was high priest and ate the loaves of offering—which it's only lawful for the priests to eat—and he gave some to those with him as well?" And he said to them, "The Sabbath was made for man, not man for the Sabbath; thus the Son of Man is Lord even of the Sabbath" (Mk 2:23-28).

Sometimes we must do things that other people disapprove of.

Occasions will arise when we must risk doing the incorrect or the unacceptable thing if we are to walk with Jesus Christ in his kingdom.

Today's Question

Can I live with people disapproving of my actions, if those actions lead to a discovery of Jesus Christ in my life?

Giftedness

You are the salt of the earth, but if the salt should lose its taste, what can it be salted with? It's good for nothing but to be thrown outside and be trampled underfoot. You are the light of the world. A city cannot be hidden, if it's set atop a mountain. Nor do you light a lamp and set it beneath a bushel; you set it on the lampstand, instead, so it gives light to everyone in the house. Let your light so shine before men that they'll see your good works and glorify your Father in Heaven (Mt 5:13-16).

Along with other segments in our society, churches call us to identify our defects, failings, inadequacies and all that goes into what we call our sinfulness. But we also need to focus on our skills, talents and virtues. We should identify and reflect on our individual giftedness.

As disciples, we have been called to honesty. Such honesty involves a willingness to accept our gifts as well as our shadows.

Today's Question

How long has it been since I thought about my giftedness?

Sensitivity

You've heard that it was said, "You shall not commit adultery!" but *I* say to you that anyone who looks at a woman with lust for her has already committed adultery with her in his heart. If your right eye causes you to sin, pull it out and throw it away from you! It's better for you to lose one part of your body than to have your whole body thrown into Gehenna. And if your right hand causes you to sin, cut it off and throw it away from you! It's better for you to lose one part of your body than to have your whole body go off to Gehenna. And it was said, "Whoever puts his wife away must give her a written notice of divorce." But *I* say to you, anyone who puts his wife away—except by reason of an unlawful union—makes her an adulteress, and whoever marries after putting her away commits adultery (Mt 5:27-32).

What may appear as insignificant or of little value to one person can be meaningful and quite valuable to another.

As disciples, we cannot presume that everybody believes, thinks, and feels as we do. We need to be sensitive to the beliefs, ideas, and practices of others, even when they appear useless to us.

Today's Question

What is one belief, idea or practice that I can show more sensitivity toward?

Unsettling

You've heard that it was said, an eye for an eye and a tooth for a tooth. But I tell you not to resist the evildoer; on the contrary, if anyone strikes you on the right cheek, turn the other to him as well; if anyone wants to go to law with you and take your tunic, give him your cloak as well, and if anyone forces you to go one mile, go with him for two. Give to those who ask of you, and don't reject those who wish to borrow from you (Mt 5:38-42).

Human responses can be settling or unsettling.

The Gospel calls us to respond to inappropriate and inhumane behavior in some unusual ways. These responses can appear strange and unsettling. However, we can be motivated to make these responses part of our attitudes and behavior if we remember how we can find the unconventional Christ in many of the unsettling events of life.

Today's Question

What is one response to abusive behavior that can be unsettling to the perpetrator?

Conversion

Once again he went out along the sea, and the whole crowd came to him and he taught them. As he walked along he saw Levi son of Alpheus seated at his tax booth, and he said to him, "Follow me!" And he got up and followed him. He reclined at table in his house, and many tax collectors and sinners were at table with Jesus and his disciples; many, indeed, were there. Also following him were scribes of the Pharisees, and when they saw that he was eating with sinners and tax collectors they said to his disciples, "Why is he eating with tax collectors and sinners?" When he heard this Jesus said to them, "The healthy aren't in need of a doctor—the sick are! I came to call sinners, not the righteous" (Mk 2:13-17).

Conversion does not take place before we encounter Jesus Christ. Rather, a genuine conversion happens when we experience Jesus Christ in our lives.

We cannot afford to believe in the mere power of our wills to bring about significant changes in our lives. Such belief places an unnecessary burden on us. It implies that we are gods.

We need to reach outside ourselves and connect with Jesus Christ before we can expect real change to occur in our lives. Therefore, as disciples, our primary task is to focus on discovering those ways by which we can connect with the Lord Jesus.

Today's Question

What is one way that I can connect with the abiding presence of Jesus Christ?

The Present

Therefore, I tell you, don't worry about your life, what you'll eat, or about your body, what you'll wear. Isn't life more than food, and the body more than clothing? Look at the birds of the sky—they neither sow nor reap nor gather into barns, yet your heavenly Father feeds them; aren't you worth more than they are? But which of you can add any time to your life by worrying? And why do you worry about clothing? Look how the lilies of the field grow; they neither work nor spin. But I tell you, even Solomon in all his glory wasn't arrayed like one of them. But if God so clothes the grass of the fields, which is here today and thrown into the oven tomorrow, won't he clothe you much better, O you of little faith? So don't go worrying, saying, "What will we eat?" or, "What will we drink?" or, "What will we put on?" for the Gentiles seek all those things. Your heavenly Father knows you need them! But first seek the Kingdom and the will of God and all those things will be given to you also. So don't go worrying about tomorrow—tomorrow will worry for itself. One day's evil is enough for a day" (Mt 6:25-34).

Yesterday has already slipped through our fingers. Tomorrow is beyond our grasp. Today is within our reach, just waiting to be embraced.

Jesus Christ moves from being a subject for historical debate or a glorious plan for the future, to a living reality when we discover him in the present. As disciples, we need to focus our energies on the events of each day so that we can live the present moment.

Today's Question

What is one worry from my past or about my future that hinders me from embracing the present?

Associates

Beware false prophets who come to you in sheep's clothing, but within are savage wolves. By their fruit you will know them! You don't gather grapes from thorns, or figs from thistles, do you? Likewise, every good tree produces good fruit, but the worthless tree produces bad fruit. A good tree can't produce bad fruit, nor can a worthless tree produce good fruit. Every tree not producing good fruit is cut down and thrown into the fire. And so, from their fruit you will know them (Mt 7:15-20).

Listen to the knowledge of the learned and the clever, but consider them wise only after you have seen them deal with life.

As disciples, we are called to harmonize our speech and our actions. Whenever possible, we should choose personal associates who give life to what they say by the way they act. It is often in our associates that we can find the Christ who can help us achieve a real harmony between our speech and our actions.

Today's Question

What is one area of disharmony that I need someone else to help me with?

Deception

Take care not to perform your good deeds in front of others in order to be seen by them; if you do, you'll have no reward from your Father in Heaven. Whenever you give alms, don't sound a trumpet before you, like the hypocrites do in the synagogues and in the streets, so people will praise them. Amen, I say to you, they have their full reward! But when you give alms, don't let your left hand know what your right hand is doing, so that your alms may be in secret, and your Father who sees in secret will reward you. And when you pray, don't be like the hypocrites—they love to pray standing in the synagogues and on the corners of wide streets, so people will notice them. Amen, I say to you, they have their full reward! But when you pray, go into your storeroom and shut the door, pray to your Father who is hidden, and your Father who sees what's hidden will reward you (Mt 6:1-6).

The more we can embrace the truth about ourselves, the less we need to be deceptive.

Putting on airs for the sake of appearances can indicate that we need to work on coming to terms with some area in ourselves.

As disciples, we need to be open with Jesus Christ so that he can help us deal with any areas of ourselves that we find unacceptable.

Today's Question

When was the last time that I put on a facade or acted in a phony manner?

Hardships

And it happened that while he was praying alone the disciples were with him, and he asked them, "Who do the crowds say I am?" In response they said, "Some say, 'John the Baptist,' while others say, 'Elijah,' and others say, 'One of the prophets of old has risen.'" Then he said to them, "But *you,* who do *you* say I am?" And in answer Peter said, "The Messiah of God!" He gave them strict orders and commanded them to tell no one about this and said, "The Son of Man must suffer greatly and be rejected by the elders and chief priests and scribes and be put to death and rise on the third day." Then he said to everyone, "If anyone would be my disciple, let him deny himself, and take up his cross daily and follow me. For whoever would save his life will lose it, while whoever loses his life for my sake, he will save it (Lk 9:18-24).

The Gospel is not a philosophy for a comfortable and carefree life. It does not provide us with information that frees us from difficulties and makes us immune to pain. Rather, the Gospel is about God entering into the stuff of human life. It is about a God who walks with us in this life, and can be found in the experiences that come our way.

In order to find Jesus Christ, we have to accept some difficulties in life. We have to embrace some sufferings. Even the wealthy and powerful people of our world, who live in mansions and palaces, find that difficulties and sufferings afflict them.

Today's Question

Am I willing to accept my difficulties and sufferings in order to find the Christ who promised to be with me?

Generosity

Large crowds followed him when he came down from the mountain and, behold, a leper came up, knelt before him, and said, "Lord, if you wish to, you can make me clean." Jesus reached out his hand, touched him, and said, "I *do* wish it, be made clean!" and at once his leprosy was made clean. Then Jesus said to him, "See that you tell no one, but go show yourself to the priest and present the offering Moses commanded, as a witness to them" (Mt 8:1-4).

True generosity reveals our personal giftedness.

We may want to be generous with our presence and our resources. This desire can be the natural result of feeling gifted with the presence of Jesus Christ. The lack of a desire to be generous can be a sign that we are not experiencing the Lord's presence. In such a case, we may need to devote more energy toward consciously discovering how Jesus Christ is gifting us with his presence.

Today's Question

When was the last time that I felt a desire to be generous?

Testimony

When he entered Capharnaum a centurion came up to him, appealing to him and saying, "Lord, my servant is lying paralyzed at home, terribly tormented." Jesus said to him, "I'll come heal him." In response the centurion said, "Lord, I'm not worthy to have you come under my roof, but just say the word and my servant will be healed. For I, too, am subject to authority and have soldiers under me, and if I say to this one, 'Go!' he goes, and if I say to another, 'Come!' he comes, and if I tell my slave, 'Do this!' he does it." When Jesus heard this he was amazed and said to those who were following, "Amen, I say to you, nowhere have I found such faith in Israel! I tell you, many will come from east and west and will recline at table with Abraham and Isaac and Jacob in the Kingdom of Heaven, but the sons of the Kingdom will be thrown out into the outer darkness; there there will be wailing and gnashing of teeth!" Then Jesus said to the centurion, "Go your way! Let it be done for you as you have believed," and his servant was healed at that very moment (Mt 8:5-13).

The overwhelming majority of people do not receive apparitions or visions from God. Most people do not have significant religious experiences every day of their lives. For the most part, we rely on our trust in the power of God's word as we go about the business of the day.

The ability to put trust in the word of God is itself a gift. However, this gift needs to be nourished if it is to fully empower us. One way that we can nourish this gift is by listening to what others have to say about Jesus Christ.

Today's Question

What is one way that I can gain more testimony about Jesus Christ?

Service

Not everyone who says to me, "Lord, Lord!" will enter the Kingdom of Heaven; no, the one who does the will of my Father in Heaven will. Many will say to me on that day, "Lord, Lord, didn't we prophesy in your name and drive out demons in your name and do mighty works in your name?" And then I'll declare to them, "I never knew you; get away from me, you evildoers!" Therefore, everyone who hears these words of mine and acts on them is like a wise man who built his house on rock. And the rain fell and the floods came and the winds blew and beat against that house, yet it didn't fall, for its foundations were set firmly on rock. Everyone who hears these words of mine and *doesn't* act on them is like a foolish man who built his house on sand. And the rain fell and the floods came, and the winds blew and beat against that house, and it fell, and great was its fall (Mt 7:21-27).

We need to allow Jesus Christ to serve us before we can serve others in his name.

We need to listen to the Gospel before we

attempt to act in the Lord's name. The Gospels reveal how the risen Lord was experienced as serving the early Church. Listening to the Gospels can help us to connect our experiences with the experiences of the first disciples. Through these connections we can discover how Jesus Christ serves us. We will then find ourselves empowered to identify how we can become genuine instruments of service to others.

Today's Question

How has Jesus Christ been of service to me?

Forgiveness

A man had two sons, and the younger of them said to his father, "Father, give me the share of the property that falls to me." Now he divided his living between them. Not many days later the younger son gathered up everything and left home for a far off country, and there he squandered his property, leading a dissolute life. When he had spent everything a severe famine came to that country and he found himself in need, so he went and attached himself to one of the citizens of that country, who sent him to his fields to feed pigs. And he longed to fill himself with the carob pods the pigs were eating, but no one gave him anything. Then, when he came to himself, he said, "How many of my father's hired men have more than enough bread, while I'm dying here of hunger. I'll get up and go to my father and I'll say to him, 'Father, I've sinned against Heaven and before you; I'm no longer worthy to be called your son; treat me like one of your hired men.'" So he got up and went to his father. While he was still far away his father saw him and took pity, and he ran and fell upon his neck and kissed him repeatedly. His son said to him, "Father, I've sinned against Heaven and before you; I'm no longer worthy to be called your son." But his father said to his servants, "Quick, bring out the best robe and clothe him in it, and put a ring on his hand and sandals on his feet, and bring the fatted calf—slaughter it and let's eat and celebrate—this son of mine was dead, and has come back to life, he was lost, and has been found." And they began to celebrate (Lk 15:11-24).

Forgiveness is not the same as forgetting. It involves more than trying to blot out a memory or erase an offense. Forgiveness goes beyond words. It cannot be fully contained in statements like: "I am sorry," or "you are forgiven." Genuine forgiveness is brought about through presence. It is a willingness to be present irrespective of an offense.

As disciples, we have been called to accept forgiveness and to forgive. We accept forgiveness when we allow those whom we have offended to be present to us, even when we can't make up for the hurt we caused them. We forgive when we are willing to be present to those who have offended us, even when we still feel the pain caused by their offenses.

Today's Question

When was the last time that I experienced forgiveness through another person's presence?

Emotions

Once again he went into the synagogue. Now a man was there who had a withered hand and they were watching closely to see whether Jesus would heal him on the Sabbath, so they could make an accusation against him. So he said to the man with the withered hand, "Stand out in the middle." Then he said to them, "Is it lawful on the Sabbath to do good or to do evil, to save a life or to put to death?" But they remained silent. And after looking around at them in anger, deeply grieved at the hardness of their hearts, he said to the man, "Hold out your hand." He held it out and his hand was restored. Then the Pharisees went out with the Herodians and began to plot to do away with Jesus (Mk 3:1-6).

Our emotions are neither good nor bad. Far from being sinful in themselves, they are simply part of being human.

We are not just rational beings. We are not computers or robots. We are also emotional beings. We need to accept our emotions, and take them with us to prayer. We need to experience a

Christ who is willing to be present to us when we are emotional. In doing so, we will experience how completely he desires to embrace us.

Today's Question

When was the last time that I became emotional or passionate about something in prayer?

Programs

This is how the Kingdom of God is, like a man who throws seed upon the earth and sleeps and rises by night and day, and the seed sprouts and grows while he's unaware. The earth bears fruit on its own, first the shoot, then the head of grain, then the full grain in the head. When it puts forth fruit he at once sends for the sickle, because the harvest has come. And he said, "How may we compare the Kingdom of God, or in what parable can we present it? It's like a grain of mustard seed which, when it's sown upon the earth, is the smallest of all the seeds on the earth, yet when it's sown it grows and becomes the biggest of all the garden plants and puts out big branches, so that the birds of the sky are able to nest in its shade" (Mk 4:26-32).

Our world is inter-connected. Something done for one person can influence many people. Something said a year ago can have an effect today.

As disciples, we are called to be with the Master. We can find this Christ dwelling within us and making himself visible in our attempts at serving others. We can also find him in those people who serve us. Sometimes, we can even find him connected to service programs that were planned and initiated long before our time here on earth.

Events in history can speak to us of the one who is Lord of history.

Today's Question

What is one service program, started years ago, that has benefited me?

Love

Now one of the Pharisees asked Jesus to eat with him, so he went into the Pharisee's house and reclined at table. There was a woman who was a sinner in the city, and when she learned that "he's reclining at table in the Pharisee's house!" she bought an alabaster jar of perfumed oil and stood behind by his feet, weeping, and she began to wet his feet with her tears and to wipe them with the hair of her head, and she kissed his feet repeatedly and anointed them with the oil. When the Pharisee who had invited him saw this he said to himself, "If this fellow were a prophet he'd have realized who and what kind of woman it is who's touching him—she's a sinner!" In response Jesus said to him, "Simon, I have something to say to you." And he said, "Teacher, say it." "Two men were debtors of a certain moneylender; the one owed five hundred denarii, the other, fifty. When they were unable to repay, he forgave them both. Which of them, then, will love him more?" In reply Simon said, "I suppose the one he forgave the most." "You've judged correctly," he said. Then turning to the woman he said to Simon, "You see this woman? I came into your house— you gave me no water for my feet, but she wet my feet with her tears and dried them with her hair. You gave me no kisses, but she, from the moment she came in, has not stopped kissing my feet. You didn't anoint my head with olive oil, but she anointed my feet with perfumed oil. Therefore I tell you: her sins, many as they are, have all been forgiven, and so she has shown great love; but whoever is forgiven little, loves little." Then he said to her, "Your sins are forgiven." And those reclining at table began to say to themselves, "Who is this fellow who even forgives sins?" Then he said to the woman, "Your faith has saved you, go in peace!" (Lk 7:36-50).

True love reveals itself by being present to another in failure and weakness.

We experience the magnitude of God's love when we discover how Jesus Christ is willing to be present to us in our sinfulness.

As disciples, we are called to look into the face of our limitations, imperfections and areas of personal sinfulness. When we discover how Christ is willing to be present in all we see, then we will discover the magnitude of God's love for us.

Today's Question

What is one area of myself that I have a difficult time accepting?

Intimidation

Behold, I'm sending you off like sheep among wolves; be as wise as serpents and guileless as doves. But beware of men—they'll hand you over to councils, and scourge you in their synagogues, and you'll be led before governors and kings for my sake, as a witness to them and to the Gentiles. But when they hand you over, don't worry about how to speak or what you should say; for what you should say will be given you in that hour, for it won't be you speaking, but the Spirit of my Father speaking in you. Brother will hand brother over to death, and father, child. And children will rebel against parents and put them to death. And you'll be hated by all because of my name, but whoever holds out till the end, they will be saved. And when they persecute you in one such city, flee to another; for, amen, I say to you, you will not finish with the cities of Israel before the Son of Man comes (Mt 10:16-23).

Intimidation drains the marrow from our souls.

As disciples, we are called to truth. However,

the truth is not always as clear as mountain spring water. Sometimes, the truth seems muddy. Circumstances can arise when it is better for us not to speak or act. At such times, we can only deal with the situation as best we can. But some situations call for action on our part even when the truth is gray and muddy. This is especially true when an individual or a group tries to victimize us by using some power to control us.

Being a disciples does not mean that we have to allow ourselves to be victimized by intimidation.

Today's Question

When was the last time that I felt intimidated?

Preconceptions

And the scribes who had come down from Jerusalem were saying, "He's possessed by Beelzebul! By the prince of demons he drives out demons!" So he called them to himself and said to them in parables, "How can Satan drive out Satan? If a kingdom is divided against itself, that kingdom is unable to stand. If a house is divided, that house will be unable to stand. And if Satan rebels against himself and is divided, he cannot last, but comes to an end. On the contrary, no one can enter the strong man's house to plunder his possessions unless he first ties the strong man up; *then* he can plunder his house. Amen, I say to you, everything will be forgiven the sons of men, their sins and the blasphemies they may blaspheme, but whoever blasphemes the Holy Spirit never has forgiveness, but is liable for an eternal sin"—because they were saying, "He has an unclean spirit!" (Mk 3:22-30)

Preconceived notions can hinder us from embracing the present.

As disciples, we need to examine and re-evaluate how and where we expect to find the Master.

Jesus Christ can reveal something of his presence through the most improbable people and in the most unfortunate events.

Today's Question

Who is one person or group of people that I don't expect Jesus Christ to work through?

Agendas

Whoever loves his father or mother more than me is not worthy of me, and whoever loves his son or daughter more than me is not worthy of me. And whoever doesn't take up his cross and follow behind me isn't worthy of me. Whoever finds his life will lose it, and whoever loses his life for my sake will find it. Whoever receives you receives me, and whoever receives me receives the One Who sent me. Whoever receives a prophet because he's a prophet shall receive a prophet's reward, and whoever receives a good man because he's a good man shall receive a good man's reward. And whoever gives even a cup of cold water to one of these little ones because he's a disciple, amen, I say to you, he will not lose his reward (Mt 10:37-42).

As disciples, we need to accept how our agendas have, in some ways, already been established by the Gospel.

We are not called to leave our families in order to be with Jesus Christ. However, we are called to look for signs of his presence in the people we love.

We are not necessarily called to leave our jobs or professions in order to find the Lord. However, we are called to discover how he is present in our work places.

Today's Question

How have I found something of Jesus Christ in someone I love?

Destruction

It happened that as the days were drawing near for Jesus to be taken up he set his face to go to Jerusalem, and he sent messengers ahead of him. They came and entered a Samaritan village to prepare for him, but the people didn't welcome him because his face was set on going to Jerusalem. When his disciples James and John saw this they said, "Lord, do you want us to call down fire from Heaven to consume them?" But he turned and rebuked them, and they went to another village (Lk 9:51-56).

The kingdom of God cannot be found in destruction for the sake of destruction.

As disciples, we need to have a plan that will allow us to build on the present before we try to destroy some part of it.

Today's Question

How can I build on something that I don't like about myself?

Schedules

As they were going along the road someone said to him, "I'll follow you wherever you go." And Jesus said to him, "Foxes have holes, and the birds of the sky have nests, but the Son of Man has nowhere to lay his head." Then he said to another, "Follow me!" "Let me first go bury my father," he said. Jesus said to him, "Let the dead bury their own dead, but *you,* go proclaim the Kingdom of God!" Then another said, "I'll follow you, Lord, but first let me take leave of those at home." But Jesus said, "No one who puts his hand to the plow and looks behind is fit for the Kingdom of God" (Lk 9:57-62).

Our schedules can crowd our lives. Our appointment books can almost enslave us. But in the midst of all our activity, we need to remember that Jesus Christ is not bound to our plans, nor is he a slave to our schedules. Jesus Christ can choose when, where and through whom he wishes to make something of himself known in the world.

Sometimes we will need to change our plans and re-arrange our schedules if we want to be with the Lord Jesus when he chooses to reveal something of his presence in our world.

Today's Question

How can I be more flexible with my schedule as I continue to discover the Lord's presence in my life?

Baggage

After this the Lord appointed seventy-two others and sent them in twos ahead of him to every town and place he was going to come to. Then he said to them, "The harvest is great, but the laborers are few, so implore the Lord of the harvest to send out laborers to his harvest. Go now! Behold, I'm sending you out like sheep among wolves. Don't carry a purse or a bag or sandals, and greet no one along the way. And to whatever house you enter, first say, 'Peace be to this house.' If there's a son of peace there your peace will rest upon him, but, if not, your peace will return to you. Stay, then, in that house and eat and drink what they have, for the laborer is worthy of his reward. Don't move from house to house. And in whatever town you enter and they receive you, eat what's set before you, heal the sick in it, and say to them, 'The Kingdom of God has come upon you!'" (Lk 10:1-9).

Excess baggage from the past prevents us from fully embracing the present.

We are who we are. Although we live in the present, we also carry the effects of past events.

But the past needn't control or diminish the present. We need to deal with our past in realistic ways. Otherwise, it becomes like excess baggage which prevents us from being with Jesus Christ in the here and now.

Today's Question

Is there something about the past that I need to deal with before I can fully live in the present?

Community

As he was walking along the Sea of Galilee he saw Simon and Simon's brother Andrew casting throw nets into the sea—they were fishermen. Jesus said to them, "Follow me, and I'll make you fishers of men!" And they left their nets at once and followed him. He continued on a little way and saw James son of Zebedee and his brother, John—they were in the boat mending the nets. He called them at once, and they left their father Zebedee in the boat with the hired men and followed him (Mk 1:16-20).

Jesus Christ does not call us to be isolated disciples relying only on our own individual resources in our endeavors. He calls us to become part of a group that grows toward him into a life of conversion and faith. We need to join with others who are also attempting to follow the Lord. This will help us discover the importance of being connected to a faith community.

Today's Question

What practical benefit have I received from being connected to my church?

Loving

And, behold, a certain lawyer stood up to put Jesus to the test and said, "Teacher, what must I do to gain eternal life?" Jesus said to him, "What's written in the Torah? How do *you* read it?" In reply he said, "You shall love the Lord your God with your whole heart and with your whole soul and with your whole strength and with your whole understanding, and you shall love your neighbor as yourself." Then Jesus said to him, "You've answered correctly; do this and you'll live." But he wished to find favor with God and so he said to Jesus, "And who *is* my neighbor?" After considering, Jesus said, "A certain man was going down from Jerusalem to Jericho and ran into robbers who, after stripping and beating him, went off leaving him half dead. Now by chance a priest was going down by that road, but when *he* saw him *he* passed by on the other side of the road. Likewise a Levite was also going past the spot, and when he saw him he passed by on the other side of the road. But a certain Samaritan who was on a journey came upon him, and when he saw him he took pity. He came up to him and bandaged his wounds, poured oil and wine on them, set him on his own mount, brought him to an inn, and took care of him. The next day when he left he gave the innkeeper two denarii and said, 'Look after him, and whatever you spend in addition I'll repay you upon my return.' Which of these three, do you think, was a neighbor to the man who ran into the robbers?" The lawyer said, "The one who had mercy on him." Then Jesus said to him, "Go, and *you* do likewise" (Lk 10:25-37).

Love reveals Jesus Christ. As disciples, loving others provides a way for us to be with Jesus Christ. We begin the process of loving through a willingness to be present to another. When we are willing to do this, we can also experience Jesus Christ. In our willingness to be present to another, the experience of Christ can help bring the process of love to its completion.

The call to love essentially focuses on the gift of our presence, and how the presence of people can reveal Jesus Christ.

Today's Question

In what way have I benefited from the presence of another human being?

Gentleness

He presented another parable to them and said, "The Kingdom of Heaven has been compared to a man who sowed good seed in his field. While everyone was sleeping his enemy came and sowed weeds among the wheat and went off, so when the shoots sprouted and bore fruit the weeds appeared then, too. The householder's servants came to him and said, 'Master, didn't you sow good seed in your field? Then where did the weeds come from?' He said to them, 'An enemy did this.' So the slaves said to him, 'Do you want us to gather them up, then?' 'No,' he said, 'you might uproot the wheat at the same time you're gathering the weeds. Let them both grow together until the harvest, and at the harvest time I'll tell the harvesters, 'First gather the weeds and tie them in bundles to be burned, but gather the wheat into my barn'" (Mt 13:24-30).

The Lord's willingness to describe us as a field that contains both weeds and wheat reveals his gentleness. He does not want to uproot all the weeds within us, because doing so would also destroy some of the wheat we possess.

As disciples, we are called to be gentle with ourselves. We may need to live with some defects, instead of trying to change them. Trying to change all of our shortcomings, or doing away with everything we don't like about ourselves can destroy some good within us.

Today's Question

What is one defect or imperfection that I need to live with so that I won't destroy some good I now possess?

Wisdom

But if God so clothes the grass of the fields, which is here today and thrown into the oven tomorrow, won't he clothe you much better, O you of little faith? So don't go worrying, saying, "What will we eat?" or, "What will we drink?" or, "What will we put on?" for the Gentiles seek all those things. Your Heavenly Father knows you need them! But first seek the Kingdom and the will of God and all those things will be given to you also. So don't go worrying about tomorrow—tomorrow will worry for itself. One day's evil is enough for a day (Mt 6:30-34).

Not knowing what to do or which way to turn is not always our fault. Sometimes, we hesitate about different aspects of life because we need information that we cannot obtain on our own. As disciples, we need to seek out and listen to the wisdom of others. Listening, instead of fear, can be the real beginning of wisdom in our lives.

Today's Question

What is one piece of valuable information that I recently received from listening to someone else?

Solitude

Then the apostles gathered around Jesus and told him all they had done and had taught. And he said to them, "Come away privately, just yourselves, to a desert place and rest for a bit." For there were so many people coming and going that they didn't even have time to eat. So they went off alone in the boat to a desert place, but the people saw them leaving and many of them found out where he was going, and they ran ahead on foot from all the towns and got there before them. When he got out of the boat he saw a large crowd, and he was moved with pity for them because they were like sheep without a shepherd, and he began to teach them many things (Mk 6:30-34).

Solitude does for a believer what the ocean does for a whale. Both provide life and the space needed to embrace it.

As disciples, we need to welcome solitude. Jesus Christ is a living person. Just as we make time to be alone with any person we want to get to know, so we need to make time to be alone with our Lord, if we want to experience him.

Sometimes we just need to give Jesus Christ some private space and time so that he can show us his presence in our lives.

Today's Question

How can I give Jesus Christ just a little more space in my life?

Liturgies

In the course of their journey Jesus entered a certain village where a woman named Martha received him. She had a sister named Mary who seated herself at the Lord's feet and listened to his teaching. But Martha was distracted with all the serving, so she came up and said, "Lord, doesn't it matter to you that my sister has left me to serve alone? Tell her to come help me!" In answer the Lord said to her, "Martha, Martha! You're anxious and upset over many things, but one thing is necessary. Mary has chosen the better part, which will not be taken from her" (Lk 10:38-42).

As disciples, we have been called to be with the Lord in liturgical prayer. In such prayer, Jesus Christ makes known to us his abiding presence.

Liturgical prayer also gives us the tools that we need to recognize how Jesus Christ reaches out to us in the people and events that shape our lives.

Today's Question

How has liturgical prayer helped me to identify Jesus Christ in my daily life?

Suffering

Then he began to teach them that the Son of Man would have to suffer greatly and be rejected by the elders and the chief priests and the scribes and be put to death and rise after three days, and he said this openly. Peter took him aside and began to remonstrate with him, but Jesus turned and, looking at his disciples, rebuked Peter and said, "Get behind me, Satan—you're not thinking the thoughts of God but of men!" Then he called the crowd to him, along with his disciples, and said to them "If anyone would be my disciple, he must deny himself and take up his cross and follow me. For whoever would save his life will lose it, and whoever loses his life for my sake and the sake of the good news will save it" (Mk 8:31-35).

Jesus did not offer his disciples any explanations for pain and sickness; nor did he promise to make them immune to suffering. Rather, by his own sufferings, Jesus opened the door through which he could enter into the place of human pain, so he could then be present to his disciples in their sufferings.

Today's Question

How has the presence of another person helped me deal with suffering?

Refreshment

At that time Jesus raised his voice and said, "I praise you, Father, Lord of heaven and earth, because you hid these things from the wise and intelligent, and revealed them to babes. Yes, Father, for such was your desire. All things have been given to me by my Father, and no one knows the Son except the Father, nor does anyone know the Father except the Son, and whomever the Son chooses to reveal him. Come to me, all you grown weary and burdened, and I will refresh you. Take my yoke upon you and learn from me, for I am gentle and humble hearted and you will find rest for your souls; for my yoke is easy, and my burden light" (Mt 11:25-30).

A hug shows us that we are lovable. An embrace reveals the warmth of a friend. When we feel disconnected and tired, we can find direction and strength from connecting with other people.

Life takes its toll on us. Difficult times can sap our strength. We may even be unable to find meaning in life.

As disciples, we have not been called to deal

with life on our own. We need other people to be part of our lives. We need to experience how Jesus Christ can refresh us through the embrace of others.

Today's Question

What is one way that I can make myself more accessible to others?

Self-Righteousness

Now the tax collectors and sinners were all drawing near to listen to him, and the Pharisees and scribes complained, "This fellow welcomes sinners and eats with them!" So he told them this parable, "What man among you who had a hundred sheep and lost one of them wouldn't leave the ninety-nine in the desert and set out after the lost one until he found it? And when he finds it he puts it on his shoulders, rejoicing, and when he comes home he calls his friends and neighbors together and says to them, 'Rejoice with me—I've found my lost sheep!' I say to you that this is the type of joy there will be in Heaven at the repentance of one sinner than at ninety-nine of the righteous who had no need of repentance. Or a woman who has ten drachmas—if she loses one drachma, won't she light a lamp and sweep her home and search thoroughly until she finds it? And when she finds it she calls her friends and neighbors and says, 'Rejoice with me, because I've found the drachma I lost!' This, I tell you, is how God's angels will rejoice over one sinner who repents" (Lk 15:1-10).

Self-righteousness, not sin, makes it difficult for us to approach Jesus Christ. As disciples, we need to acknowledge that we are not complete, and that we are incapable of making ourselves complete. Such self-righteousness hinders us from being with Jesus Christ.

We can't earn the presence of Jesus Christ in our lives. It is a gift. The discovery of this gift in the midst of personal failure gives us the strength we need to deal with our limitations.

Today's Question

Is there some defect or limitation that I am trying to overcome without any help from others, including Jesus Christ?

The Ordinary

The Kingdom of Heaven is like a treasure hidden in a field which a man found and hid, and in his joy he went off and sold all he had and bought that field. Again, the Kingdom of Heaven is like a merchant seeking fine pearls; when he found one very precious pearl he went and sold off all he had and bought it (Mt 13:44-46).

Our encounters with Jesus Christ do not always involve an arresting or gripping event. Sometimes, Christ chooses to make himself known to us through the ordinary happenings in our lives.

Discovering how Jesus Christ is present in everyday events can make them significant. Embracing the ordinary by spending time with it, instead of running away from it, can lead to such a discovery.

Today's Question

What recent event in my life appeared to be ordinary at first but took on a significant meaning with time?

Faith

So when the crowd saw that neither Jesus nor his disciples were there they got into the boats and went to Capharnaum in search of Jesus. And when they found him on the other side of the sea they said, "Rabbi, when did you come here?" Jesus answered them and said, "Amen, amen, I say to you, you seek me not because you saw signs, but because you ate of the loaves and were satisfied. Labor not for food that perishes, but for food that remains for life eternal, which the Son of Man will give you, for God the Father has set his seal on him." So they said to him, "What should we do to do the works of God?" Jesus answered and said to them, "This is the work of God, to believe in the one he sent." So they said to him, "Then what sign do you do, so we can see and believe in you? What work do you perform? Our fathers ate manna in the desert, as it is written, 'he gave them bread from Heaven to eat.'" Jesus said to them, "Amen, amen, I say to you, it wasn't Moses who gave you bread from Heaven; on the contrary, my Father gives you the true bread from Heaven, for God's bread is the bread that comes down from Heaven and gives life to the world." So they said to him, "Lord, give us this bread always." Jesus said to them, *"I* am the bread of life; whoever comes to me shall not hunger, and whoever believes in me shall never thirst" (Jn 6:24-35).

Faith in anything or anyone does not come about without hard work.

As disciples, we are called to faith in Jesus Christ. We are called to believe that he rose from the dead and promised to be with us until the end of time. We are called to trust in the power of his presence. However, such faith does not come about in us on its own. It takes work!

We need to work at listening to God's word. We need to work at making time for God in our lives. We need to work at being attentive to the signs of Christ's presence in our world. We need to work at being with others who are also trying to believe in Jesus Christ.

Today's Question

What is one work of faith that I need to spend more time with?

Greed

Then someone from the crowd said to him, "Teacher, tell my brother to share the inheritance with me!" But he said to him, "Man, who made me judge or arbitrator over you?" Then he said to them, "Watch out for and guard against all greed, because your life doesn't consist in the abundance of your possessions." Then he told them a parable and said, "The land of a certain rich man produced good crops. So he considered to himself, 'What shall I do—I have nowhere to gather my grain! This is what I'll do,' he said, 'I'll pull down my barns and build bigger ones, and I'll gather all my grain and my goods there, and I'll tell my soul, "Soul, you have many goods laid up for many years. Relax; eat, drink, be merry!"' But God said to him, 'You fool! This night they'll demand your soul of you. But the things you prepared, whose will *they* be?' That's how it will be for whoever accumulates treasure for himself, yet is not generous toward God" (Lk 12:13-21).

Wealth is not evil! In many cases, it results from determination or hard work, neither of which can be called evil. However, wealth cannot become the focal point of our lives. As disciples, we are called to be much more than wealthy individuals. We are called to be with the Lord and Savior of the world. We can use wealth to help us find something of the Christ. But we must never allow it to hinder us in our quest for union with Jesus Christ.

Today's Question

How can I use wealth to find something of Jesus in my world?

Touched

At once he made his disciples get into the boat and go on ahead of him to the other side while he sent the crowds away, and after sending the crowds away he went up the mountain to pray in private. When evening came on he was there alone, while the boat was already several miles away from land, tossed about by the waves, for the wind was against it. Shortly before dawn he came toward them, walking on the sea. When the disciples saw him walking on the sea they were terrified and said, "It's a ghost!" and they cried out in fear. But he spoke to them at once and said, "Take courage! It's me! Don't be afraid!" In answer to him Peter said, "Lord, if it's you, command me to come to you on the water." "Come!" he said. Peter got out of the boat and began to walk on the water and drew near to Jesus, but when he saw the wind he became frightened and, as he began to sink, he cried out and said, "Save me, Lord!" At once Jesus reached out his hand and caught him and said to him, "O you of little faith, why did you doubt?" And when they got into the boat the wind ceased.

Those in the boat worshipped him and said, "Truly you're the Son of God!" (Mt 14:22-33)

Jesus Christ does not demand perfection before he enters our lives. He is willing to touch us when we sin and lift us up when we fail.

As disciples, we are called to experience a Christ who is willing to touch us when we sin and embrace us when we fail. We need such experiences if we are to believe the Good News. Such experiences can be ours if we attempt to be genuine or real when we place ourselves in the presence of the Lord.

Today's Question

Is there something about myself that I fear to bring out into the open when I am with Jesus Christ?

Fear

Fear not, little flock for it pleased your Father to give you the Kingdom. Sell your possessions and give alms; make yourselves purses that don't grow old, an inexhaustible treasure in the heavens, where no thief approaches nor moth destroys; for where your treasure is, there will your heart be, too! Let your loins be girt and your lamps burning, and you like men awaiting their lord, when he at last returns from the wedding feast, so when he comes and knocks they can open up for him at once. Blessed those servants who, when he comes, the lord will find still awake! Amen I say to you, he'll get himself dressed and have them recline at table, and he'll come wait on them. And if he comes in the middle of the night and finds them thus, they are blessed! But know this—if the householder had known at what hour the thief was coming he wouldn't have let his house be broken into. You be ready, too, because you don't know the hour when the Son of Man is coming! (Lk 12:32-40)

Some things in life are better left undone until tomorrow. However, if out of fear we put off something that needs to be done today, then we give fear the power to master our lives.

Jesus Christ can bring us to a fuller life by helping us deal with our fears. We need to go to the Lord Jesus when fear strikes us. Jesus gives us the courage and strength to embrace our fears when we face them in his presence. Facing our fears diminishes the power they have over us. They will no longer control our lives.

Today's Question

What is one fear that I need to take to Jesus Christ?

Happiness

Jesus said: "The Son of Man must suffer greatly and be rejected by the elders and chief priests and scribes and be put to death and rise on the third day." Then he said to everyone, "If anyone would be my disciple, he must deny himself, and take up his cross daily and follow me. For whoever would save his life will lose it, while whoever loses his life for my sake, he will save it. For what good is it if you gain the whole world, but lose or forfeit your life?" (Lk 9:22-25)

Happiness is not the mere absence of difficulties. Rather, true happiness can be found in an obstacle that has been embraced, presented to God, shared with others and lived with.

Today's Question

What is one difficulty that I need to present to the Lord?

Peacefulness

I came to spread fire on the earth, and would that it were already kindled! But I have a baptism to be baptized with, and how apprehensive I am until it is accomplished! Do you think I came to bring peace to the earth? No, I tell you, but division instead! For from now on five in one house will be divided, three against two and two against three, father against son will be divided and son against father, mother against daughter and daughter against mother, mother-in-law against daughter-in-law and daughter-in-law against mother-in-law (Lk 12:49-53).

Our experiences of Jesus Christ do not necessarily banish conflict or division from our lives. However, they can enable us to be at peace with conflict and division. This peace is a gift we receive from being with the Lord. The yearning for such peace is one way that the Lord calls us to himself.

Today's Question

Is there some conflict in my life that I would be better off learning to live with instead of trying to change?

Impacting

When he left there Jesus withdrew to the district of Tyre and Sidon. And, behold, a Canaanite woman from that region came and cried out, "Have mercy on me, Lord, Son of David! My daughter is severely tormented by a demon!" But not a word did he answer her. His disciples came and begged him, saying, "Send it away—she keeps crying out behind us!" But in reply he said, "I was sent only to the lost sheep of the house of Israel." So the woman came and knelt before him and said, "Lord, help me!" In reply he said, "It isn't right to take the children's bread and throw it to the pups." But she said, "O yes, Lord—even the pups eat the crumbs that fall from their masters' table!" In answer, then, Jesus said to her, "O woman, great is your faith! Let it be done for you as you wish!" And her daughter was healed from that very hour (Mt 15:21-28).

Faith in Jesus Christ makes a decisive difference in our lives. It influences the way we approach life and teaches us how to deal with it. It influences the expectations we place on life, and can even determine the depth to which we experience life.

Today's Question

How has my faith influenced the way that I deal with life?

Immortality

So the Jews complained about him because he said, "I am the bread come down from Heaven," and they said, "Isn't this fellow Jesus son of Joseph? Don't we know his father and mother? How can he now say, 'I've come down from Heaven?'" Jesus answered and said to them, "Don't complain among yourselves. No one can come to me unless the Father who sent me draws him, and I'll raise him up on the last day. It is written in the Prophets, 'and they will all be taught by God.' Everyone who listens to the Father and learns, comes to me. Not that anyone has seen the Father except the one who is from the Father; *he* has seen the Father. Amen, amen, I say to you, whoever believes has eternal life. *I* am the bread of life. Your fathers ate manna in the desert yet they died. This is the bread that came down from Heaven, so that you can eat of it and *not* die. I am the living bread that came down from Heaven. If anyone eats of this bread he'll live forever, but the bread that *I'll* give for the life of the world is my flesh" (Jn 6:41-51).

We may possess powerful abilities or talents. We may even accomplish lofty goals. However, we cannot completely satisfy our basic drive for immortality.

As disciples, we spend time with Jesus Christ and trust him to give us what we cannot give ourselves. We turn to him for the gift of life beyond the grave. We turn to him to take care of the future so that we can fully embrace the present.

Today's Question

Am I prevented from fully living my present life because I fear to trust Jesus Christ with my future immortality?

Relaxation

Then the apostles gathered around Jesus and told him all they had done and had taught. And he said to them, "Come away privately, just yourselves, to a desert place and rest for a bit." For there were so many people coming and going that they didn't even have time to eat. So they went off alone in the boat to a desert place, but the people saw them leaving and many of them found out where he was going, and they ran ahead on foot from all the towns and got there before them. When he got out of the boat he saw a large crowd, and he was moved with pity for them because they were like sheep without a shepherd, and he began to teach them many things (Mk 6:30-34).

"I feel as if life is crushing me!" "I feel like the demands of my life have knocked the breath out of me!" When we can relate to one or both of these statements, then it is time for us to go to our own out of-the-way place without feeling guilty about it.

The Lord often calls us to relax in his presence. Sometimes that call comes in the feeling of being overwhelmed. Let us recognize it for what it is and respond to it.

Today's Question

Where is my out-of-the-way place where I can rest with my Lord?

Foolishness

Then some one from the crowd said to him, “Teacher, tell my brother to share the inheritance with me!” But he said to him, “Man, who made me judge or arbitrator over you?” Then he said to them, “Watch out for and guard against all greed, because your life doesn’t consist in the abundance of your possessions.” Then he told them a parable and said, “The land of a certain rich man produced good crops. So he considered to himself, ‘What shall I do—I have nowhere to gather my grain! This is what I’ll do,’ he said, ‘I’ll pull down my barns and build bigger ones, and I’ll gather all my grain and my goods there, and I’ll tell my soul, “Soul, you have many goods laid up for many years. Relax; eat, drink, be merry!”’ But God said to him, ‘You fool! This night they’ll demand your soul of you. But the things you prepared, whose will *they* be?’ That’s how it will be for whoever accumulates treasure for himself, yet is not generous toward God” (Lk 12:13-21).

Some things in life are not worth dying for. Life is a delicate and precious gift. In life, we are called to discern what is truly worth the price of our lives, and what falls short of such a price.

Today's Question

What is one thing that I would like to have that is not worth dying for?

Practices

Now when Jesus came to the district of Caesarea Philippi he began to question his disciples, "Who do they say the Son of Man is?" "Some say John the Baptist," they said, "others, Elijah, still others, Jeremiah or one of the prophets." Then he asked them, "But who do *you* say I am?" Peter replied, "You're the Messiah, the Son of the Living God!" In response Jesus said to him, "Blessed are you, Simon bar Jonah, for it wasn't flesh and blood that revealed this to you, but my Father in Heaven. And now I tell you, that you are Peter, and on this rock I will build my church, and the gates of hell will not prevail against it. I will give you the keys of the Kingdom of Heaven, and whatever you bind on earth will have been bound in Heaven, and whatever you loose on earth will have been loosed in Heaven." Then he ordered the disciples not to tell anyone that he was the Messiah (Mt 16:13-20).

We need to encounter Jesus Christ before we can genuinely proclaim him to be Lord. We need to listen to the Sacred Scriptures and join others for communal prayer and liturgical worship. These practices enable us to identify how Jesus Christ is already present in our lives. They give us the direction and insight we need to encounter his presence. It is by encountering the Lord's presence in our lives that we are then empowered to echo the declaration: "Jesus Christ is the Messiah, the Son of the living God!"

Today's Question

What is one way that I can be more attentive to the scriptures?

Determination

Many of his disciples who were listening said, "This teaching is hard; who can accept it?" Now Jesus knew in himself that his disciples were complaining about this and he said to them, "Does this offend you? What if you see the Son of Man ascending to where he was before? The Spirit is the life-giver, the flesh is profitless; the words I speak to you are Spirit and are life. But there are some of you who don't believe." For Jesus knew from the beginning who they were who didn't believe, and who it was who would hand him over. And he said, "This is why I told you that no one can come to me unless it's given to him by the Father." Because of this, many of his disciples turned back and no longer walked with him. So Jesus said to the Twelve, "Do you, too, wish to turn back?" Simon Peter answered him, "Lord, who would we go to? You have the words of eternal life, and we've believed and come to know that you're the Holy One of God" (Jn 6:60-69).

The words of Sacred Scripture do not necessarily affirm us in our present beliefs or practices.

They are not intended to give us warm fuzzy feelings. Rather, they are intended to speak to our faith. In doing so, the words we hear will sometimes challenge us and may even disturb us.

We may not always find that the words of the scriptures appeal to or inspire us. Sometimes it takes determination to stay with the scriptures and allow them to speak to our faith. However, such determination can be found if we view the scriptures as a way by which we can spend time with Jesus Christ.

Today's Question

What is one passage from Sacred Scripture that I don't like to hear?

Forgiving

Then Peter came and said to him, "Lord, how many times can my brother sin against me and I'll have to forgive him? Up to seven times?" Jesus said to him, "I don't say to you up to seven times, but instead up to seventy seven-times. Therefore, the Kingdom of Heaven may be compared to a king who wanted to settle accounts with his servants. When he began settling up a debtor was brought to him who owed ten thousand talents. Since the man was unable to repay the debt the lord ordered him to be sold, along with his wife and children and everything he had, and payment made. The servant fell down, therefore, knelt before the king, and said, 'Be patient with me and I'll pay you back everything!' Deeply moved, the lord of that servant released him and forgave him the debt. But when that servant went out he found one of his fellow servants who owed him a hundred denarii, and he grabbed him and started choking him and said, 'Pay back what you owe!' The fellow servant fell down and pleaded with him, saying, 'Be patient with me and I'll pay you back!' But he wouldn't listen; instead, he went and threw him into prison until he could pay back what was owed. When his fellow servants saw what had happened they were terribly distressed, and they went and told their lord everything that had happened. Then the lord summoned the servant and said to him, 'You wicked servant! I forgave you all that debt when you begged me; shouldn't you have had mercy on your fellow servant, too, as I had mercy on you?' And in his anger the lord handed him over to the jailers until he could pay back all that was owed. That's what my Heavenly Father will do to you, too, unless each of you forgives your brother from your heart" (Mt 18:21-35).

We have not been called to forgive others in order to make ourselves worthy of God, or to earn the friendship of a God who is distant from us. As disciples, we have been called to forgive those who do us wrong. Doing so reveals the spark of the divine that is already present within us. The action of forgiving enables us to encounter the Christ who dwells within us.

Today's Question

Who is one person whom I need to forgive?

Sinners

Now the tax collectors and sinners were all drawing near to listen to him, and the Pharisees and scribes complained, "This fellow welcomes sinners and eats with them!" So he told them this parable, "What man among you who had a hundred sheep and lost one of them wouldn't leave the ninety-nine in the desert and set out after the lost one until he found it? And when he finds it he puts it on his shoulders, rejoicing, and when he comes home he calls his friends and neighbors together and says to them, 'Rejoice with me—I've found my lost sheep!' I say to you that this is the type of joy there will be in Heaven at the repentance of one sinner than at ninety-nine of the righteous who had no need of repentance. Or a woman who has ten drachmas—if she loses one drachma, won't she light a lamp and sweep her home and search thoroughly until she finds it? And when she finds it she calls her friends and neighbors and says, 'Rejoice with me, because I've found the drachma I lost!' This, I tell you, is how God's angels will rejoice over one sinner who repents" (Lk 15:1-10).

The Gospel is not a how-to-book for bringing about our salvation. It has no magic formulas for making God present in our lives. The Gospel reveals the salvation that is already taking place. It is about the Christ who is already present to us.

The Good News of Jesus Christ speaks to us of the God who is willing to sit down at table with us, even when we sin. Our lives change and take on a new perspective when we discover how Christ is willing to be present to us in all we experience, even the experience of sin.

Today's Question

How have I experienced the willingness of Jesus Christ to be present to me when I sin?

Family

He went to the other side of the sea to the region of the Gerasenes, and when he got out of the boat he was confronted by a man with an unclean spirit who came up to him from among the tombs. This man lived among the tombs and no one was able to restrain him, even with chains—he'd been put in chains and restrained many times, yet he'd broken the chains and restraints to bits and scattered them, and no one was able to control him. He spent all night and day among the tombs and on the mountains, shouting and cutting himself with stones. When he caught sight of Jesus from a distance, he rushed up and fell on his knees before him, crying out in a loud voice, "What do you want with me, Jesus, Son of the Most High God? I beg you in the name of God not to torment me!" because Jesus had been saying to him, "Come out of the man, unclean spirit!" Jesus asked him, "What's your name?" and he said to him, "My name is Legion, because there are many of us." And he kept begging Jesus not to send them out of the region. Now there was a large herd of swine on the hillside there, feeding, and they begged him, "Send us into the swine; let us enter into them!" So he gave them permission and when the unclean spirits had gone out they went into the swine, and the herd, numbering about two thousand, rushed headlong down the slope into the sea and was drowned. The men who had been feeding them fled and spread the news in the town and the fields, and the people came to see what had happened. When they came up to Jesus and saw the demon-possessed man sitting there, clothed and in his right mind—the one who had been possessed by Legion—they became frightened. Then those who had seen it all told them how this had come about for the demon-possessed man, and also about the swine. And the people began to beg Jesus to leave their district. When he had gotten into the boat the man who had been demon-possessed begged him to let him go with him, but he wouldn't allow him to; instead he told him, "Go off to your home, to your own people, and proclaim to them everything the Lord has done for you and how he had mercy on you." So he went off and began to proclaim in the Decapolis what Jesus had done for him, and they were all astounded (Mk 5:1-20).

As disciples, we are eventually called to join Jesus Christ in proclaiming the Good News of the kingdom. However, few of us are called to go out preaching the Gospel to a large community. Most of us are called to focus our efforts on our families.

Within our families, we do not usually preach Jesus through formal doctrinal instruction. Rather, we become living testimonials to the difference that Jesus Christ can make in people's lives. The personal encounters we have with Jesus Christ bring about these differences in us. So we need to spend time with the Lord so that we can become genuine testimonials of the Good News to our families.

Today's Question

Is there someone in my family who reminds me of the difference that Jesus Christ can make in human life?

The Body

A large crowd was following Jesus and kept crowding in on him. Now a woman was there who had had a heavy flow of blood for twelve years and had suffered greatly at the hands of many doctors. She'd spent all she had but had nothing to show for it; on the contrary, her condition was getting worse. Having heard about Jesus, she came with the crowd and touched his cloak from behind, because she said, "If I can just touch even part of his cloak I'll be saved." At once her flow of blood dried up, and she knew in her body that she was cured from the illness. Jesus himself realized at once that power had gone out from him and he turned around in the crowd saying, "Who touched my cloak?" His disciples said to him, "You see the crowd pressing in on you! How can you say, 'Who touched me?'" But he kept looking around to see who had done it. Then the woman, trembling and afraid because she knew what had happened to her, came and fell down before him and told him the whole truth. But he said to her, "Daughter, your faith has saved you; go in peace and be cured of your illness" (Mk 5:24-34).

The eternal Word of God did not enter our world as a human being just to save our souls. Jesus Christ sanctified the body by joining the divine to the human in his own person. He showed genuine concern and great respect for the human body throughout his earthly ministry.

As disciples, we can join Jesus Christ in his mission to humanity by respecting the human body. We can even discover how the Lord connects with us through our efforts to care for our bodies.

Today's Question

What is one way that I can show more respect for my body?

Co-Dependency

Jesus left there and came to his hometown, and his disciples followed him. When the Sabbath came he began to teach in the synagogue, and most of those who were listening were amazed and said, "Where did this fellow get all this? What sort of wisdom has been given to him that such mighty works should come about at his hands? Isn't this the carpenter, the son of Mary and the brother of James and Joses and Judas and Simon? Aren't his sisters right here among us?" And they rejected him. Jesus said to them, "A prophet is without honor only in his hometown and among his kinsmen and in his own house." He was unable to do any mighty works there, except that he cured a few sick people by laying his hands on them, and he was astounded at their unbelief (Mk 6:1-6).

It is one thing for us to drag around our personal baggage from the past. However, it is entirely something else when we insist on carrying other people's baggage along with our own.

We can deal with our past so that it does not prevent us from fully living the present. But we cannot deal with the past for others. We can help them with guidance and support, but we cannot fix their lives for them. We do not have the power to be gods in other people's lives. They must deal with the past themselves. They must even be willing to ask God for help, before he can give them the help that they need.

Today's Question

What is one way that I have tried to fix other people's lives?

Connecting

Then he went around the surrounding villages teaching. He summoned the Twelve and began to send them out two by two, and he gave them authority over the unclean spirits and ordered them to take nothing on the road except a staff—not bread, not a bag, nor money in their belts—but instead to put sandals on their feet and not to wear two tunics. And he said to them, "Wherever you enter a house, stay there until you leave the place. But if any place doesn't receive you or give you a hearing, when you're leaving there shake the dust from the soles of your feet in witness against them." So they went out and proclaimed that the people should repent, and they drove out many demons and anointed many sick people with oil and cured them (Mk 6:7-13).

At times we may feel called to offer our service to an individual or a group. If such a call is truly from the Lord Jesus, then there is a good possibility that we are also being called to join ourselves to at least one other person who can aid us in such service. The Lord Jesus does not normally call us to venture upon some act of service in total isolation from others.

As disciples, we are called to join ourselves to others in what we do for the sake of God's kingdom. We are empowered to act in the name of Jesus Christ by connecting ourselves to other believers in the Church. Jesus Christ then strengthens us to complete our mission of service when he reveals his abiding presence through the connections that we make with others.

Today's Question

What is one act of service in which I can use some help?

Speech

Herod himself had sent and had John seized and kept him in prison because of Herodias, the wife of his brother Philip, because he'd married her. For John had been telling Herod, "It isn't lawful for you to have your brother's wife." Now Herodias held this against John and wanted to have him killed, but she was unable to because Herod feared John, knowing him to be an upright and holy man. So he kept an eye on him and when he listened to him he was greatly disturbed, and yet he liked to listen to him. But a day of opportunity came for Herodias when Herod held a feast for his top men and the tribunes and the most important men from Galilee, and when Herodias' own daughter came in and danced she pleased Herod and the guests. The king said to the girl, "Ask me whatever you want and I'll give you it," and he swore to her, "Whatever you ask me for I'll give you, up to half my kingdom." She went out and said to her mother, "What should I ask for?" And her mother said, "The head of John the Baptizer." So she hurried in at once to the king and made her request—"I want you to give me, right now, the head of John the Baptist on a platter." The king was greatly distressed; because of the oaths and the guests he didn't want to refuse her, so the king sent at once and ordered an executioner to bring John's head. The executioner went off and beheaded John in the prison, and he brought the head on a platter and gave it to the girl, and she gave it to her mother. And when his disciples heard they came and carried the corpse away and laid it in a tomb (Mk 6:17-29).

Honesty is food for the soul. Deceit robs us of worth. Promises are to be made with great care, and oaths should be taken only when needed, for irresponsible words can endanger our integrity. We can deprive our future of joy by a simple phrase in the present. We can find something of Jesus Christ in words that are spoken to us. We can find ourselves being connected to Jesus Christ in the words that we speak to others.

Today's Question

What is one way that I can be more responsible with my speech?